a worker's manifesto to slacking off

a worker's manifesto to slacking off:

52 Outrageous Office Games to Keep You Sane (and Drive Your Boss Crazy!)

Annie **Jackson**

Copyright © 2010 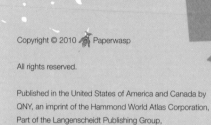 Paperwasp

Published in the United States of America and Canada by
QNY, an imprint of the Hammond World Atlas Corporation,
Part of the Langenscheidt Publishing Group,
Long Island City, NewYork
www.langenscheidt.com

QNY and the QNY colophon are trademarks of the American Map Corporation.

Catalog-in-Publication data is available from the Library of Congress

This book was conceived, designed, and produced by
Paperwasp, an imprint of Balley Design Limited,
The Mews, 16 Wilbury Grove, Hove, East Sussex, BN3 3JQ, U.K.
www.paperwaspbooks.com

Creative director: Simon Balley
Designer: Andrew Li
Project editor: Kathy Steer
Cover design: Simon Balley
Illustrations: Andrew Li

ISBN: 978-0841-671997

Printed in China

Contents

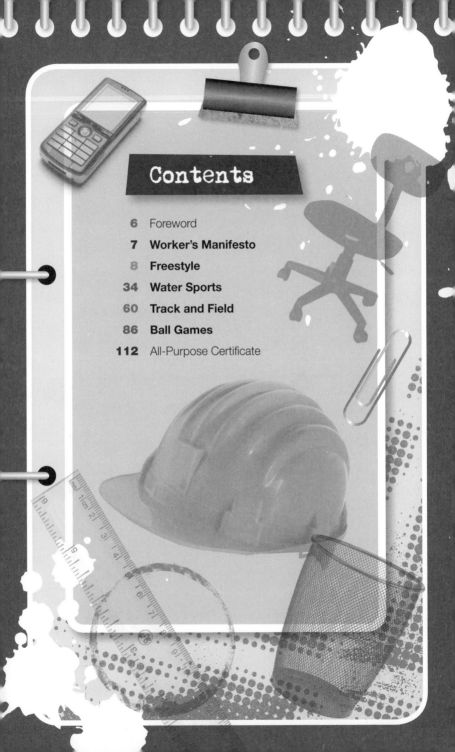

Foreword

Times are tough, the economy's in the crapper, you're working harder than you signed on for and the Man is squeezing every last drop out of us stressed out, insecure, beleaguered employees because he can, but even middle management is facing tough times, with downturns and cutbacks. What can an average slacker do to blow off a little steam during the 9–5 struggle? How can we screw the system without screwing ourselves?

The Worker's Manifesto shows the way forward: 52 physically and mentally challenging activities (using only office equipment and supplies) to suit all abilities, divided into four categories for you to mix and match as suits your office environment and staff levels. Everything you need is here—rules, equipment list, course specifications, number of contenders and officials, and even an official Worker's Manifesto fun stat panel, which we have called WM stats, to keep you motivated. We have even supplied a certificate (photocopy and fill in as required) and cut-out-and-keep medals. If challenged by a Capitalist Bootlicker or Running Dog of Wall Street, point out that you are saving the company thousands of dollars and worker hours since they won't need to send anyone on team building courses or bonding retreats ever again.

Worker's Manifesto

Workers of the office world unite!
Free yourselves from cubicle serfdom!
Stop the insidious spread of bureaucratic boredom!
You are not a number!

● You have a right to have fun!

● You have a right to stay sane and healthy even at work!

● You have a right to control the means of production in a creative manner!

● You have a right to fight against the daily grind!

● You have nothing to lose but your fat butt/muffin top/beer gut!

Butt Photocopying Time Trials

Once regarded as an amateur pastime, this popular event now enjoys professional status as photocopying technology has developed.

Object >> to set up machine and photocopy as many copies of your bare butt as possible within specified time (usually 10 minutes)

Players >> this is a solo event

Course >> Use static, free-standing, waist-height, standard photocopier for the best results.

Equipment >>
● One photocopier *(any model)*
● 8 ½ ins x 11 ins paper
● Toner
● Glass cleaner

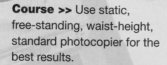

Rules >>

● slackers must load up machine with paper and toner

● butts must be completely bare

● butts must be clearly defined on each copy

● paper jams must be cleared by competitor alone

● time taken to clear a jam will count as part of the trial

If you play Connecticut Rules, sheets should be collated and stapled in threes.

Officials >>
● timekeeper
● quality checker

Level of fitness >>

	high
	med
✓	low

WM stat >>

The World Record (198 8 ½ ins x 11 ins b/w sheets in 10 minutes) is held by P.J. Witherspoon, a White House intern during the Bill Clinton era.

freestyle

9

Free Running Trials

A sport that started in the suburbs of Paris, France, has now gone mainstream and moved indoors. It can be easily justified to management as an at-work initiative training exercise. You may have to let the more gym-obsessed bosses join in.

Object >> to move about the office all day without touching the ground

Players >> this is a solo event, although can also be played as a tag team of maximum four members

Course >> Any part or all of the office, and beyond, to be agreed beforehand (e.g., decide whether or not to include restrooms). No previous setting up of helpful objects is allowed, but runners may adjust office furniture as they go round. All office furniture, walls and architectural features may be used.

Equipment >>
● no extra equipment (e.g., crutches, skateboards) is allowed

Rules >>

- competitors must all start on the whistle

- wheeled chairs may not be used for seated travel but can form part of a run, and may be stood on

- time points awarded for ingenuity and daring

- runners must not touch floor with hands or feet

- runners must not be carried by non-runners but may bounce off them

- runners must have their own insurance

Officials >>
- umpire

Level of fitness >>

✓	high
	med
	low

WM stat >>

In 2003, Jonathan "The Cat" Kowalski, a credit card call center employee, ran his company's entire building for three shifts and solved a restroom problem by going in through the ventilation duct in the ceiling and bouncing off the shoulders of his unsuspecting supervisor onto the sink.

freestyle

Office Chair Curling

Chair curling was being played long before standard curling became an Olympic sport (1998) because it can be easily played right under the boss's nose. Management, usually being myopic, will assume you are the new cleaning crew.

Object >> To slide stones (CD spindle packs) along the floor to the target (or *house*) getting it as near the center as possible to score points. Blocking and bumping opponents' stone is a key strategy in game play. Most points after four attempts per team wins.

Players >> two teams of two slackers, one to launch the stone, the other to sweep the path before it

Equipment >>
● 2 wheeled office chairs for sweepers
● curling stones (up to 8); made from CD spindle packs (the kind with a lid) weighted for play
● 2 brooms
● masking tape to mark out target, starting line and hog line

● One player launches the stone
● The other player is the sweeper and plays by SITTING ON THEIR WHEELED CHAIR zooming along ahead of the stone, but slightly to the side.

Course, or Sheet >> long passageway or corridor with smooth noncarpeted floor. Area needs to be big enough to mark off a start line, a hog line, or foul line, and a *house*, or target area.

Rules >>

● player delivering stone must sit at all times, but can lean in any direction

● player must launch stone at starting line and have removed his/her hand by the time it reaches hog line (4 ft further along)

● sweeper must travel sideways along the course, sweeping as he/she goes

● each team takes turns delivering stones; best of eight wins

● wool beanies and gloves must be worn

Officials >>
● umpire
● scorekeeper

Level of fitness >>

	high
✓	med
	low

WM stat >>

Curling has been banned in Indiana since 2002 after Senator Betsy Macbeth had her ankle (and the high heel of her Louboutin) shattered by an overenthusiastic curler at the Potter-Pirbright Paper Company, South Bend, when she was on a fact-finding mission.

freestyle

Water Cooler Bowling

This can only be played with the co-operation of your janitorial/maintenance department— offering a great opportunity to foster workplace solidarity between white- and blue-collar staff.

Object >> To knock down all the pins (empty watercooler bottles), either all at once or in a sequence, just like real bowling. If you play Body Bowling, you ball yourself up in the fetal position and roll yourself at the pins.

Players >> can be played as individuals or in teams

Alley >> Four (minimum) lanes with room for the pins at one end. Lanes can be separated by rows of desks.

Equipment >>
- ten empty watercooler bottles
- bowling balls made from padded envelopes weighted with hole punches and stuffed with shredded unused promotional postcards
- masking tape to mark start line

Rules >>

● bowlers must choose Body or classic mode and stick to it

● if playing Body Bowling, "ball" must be self-propelled, not thrown by another player

● pins must be set up in the standard 1-2-3-4 bowling pin formation

● bowlers play ten frames

● scoring is the same as in traditional bowling

Officials >>
● scorekeeper

Level of fitness >>

	high
✓	med
	low

WM stat >>

In 2005 the winning Body Bowling team from Miami Mutual & Savings took the game outside the office and started their own Beach Body Bowling League. A cable TV deal is on the table.

freestyle

Office Jousting

Jousting was a medieval display sport not unlike World Wrestling Entertainment today. If you work in the creative industry, you might persuade your boss that this is an imaginative way for teams to compete for accounts, projects, etc.

Object >> to unseat your opponent from his mount (office chair) using a lance (mailing tube); there are three passes, best of three wins

Players >> four to 10 teams of two (squire and knight)

Lists >> long passageway or corridor with enough room for two chairs to pass comfortably with a central dividing line and midpoint marker clearly indicated

Equipment >>
● heavy, wheeled office chair
● padded envelope armor (breastplate, knee pads, gauntlets)
● trashcan helmet with paper plume
● double thickness cardboard shield decorated with knight's coat of arms

● lance (long cardboard tube, tapered, reinforced with duct tape)
● masking tape to make both a central dividing line and a midpoint line

Rules >>

● knights may be pushed by squires to get momentum, but squires must release 5 yds from midpoint line

● knights must not cross over their own boundary line

● if lances miss, it is deemed a mis-joust and must be taken again

● no kicking or elbowing

Officials >>
● umpire
● chairwheel smith
● armorer

Level of fitness >>

✓	high
	med
	low

WM stat >>

Jousting is popular with the geekerati (who spend a lot of time jousting online as Elf Lords), so it is no surprise that Apple's Sir Travis de Slacker (the "Snow Leopard") has been Top Knight for the last two jousting seasons.

freestyle

Paperclip Archery

A quiet game that can be played in spare moments; an archery tournament can go on for months if necessary. If questioned, remind the management that you have a constitutional right to bear arms at any time.

Object >> to shoot as many bull's eyes as possible using handmade miniature bows

Archers >> as many as want to enter the tournament

Range >> stick targets at eye height on walls or filing cabinets and allow 10 yds space in front for archers to take shot

Equipment >>
● paperclips, rubber bands for bows
● lightweight ballpoint pens or similar for arrows
● paper targets
● masking tape to mark toe lines (where archer must stand to take shot)

Rules >>

- archers must make their own bows and arrows

- archers may compete sitting or standing

- bows and arrows must be inspected before use

- arrows need not penetrate; where they hit must be marked and initialed

•• Use large paperclip. Unbend, leaving curvature; bend ends back to make hooks. String with small rubber bands. Take out ink tube from ballpoint open; stick paper feathers at blunt end, and replace pointy cap to make arrowhead.

Officials >>
- scorekeeper
- target manager

Level of fitness >>

	high								
	med								
✓	low								

WM stat >>

The Robin Hood of paperclip archery is R. Otis Loxley of stationery megacorps G.D. Gisburn of Nottingham, Pennsylvania, who hit 24 bull's eyes in succession in the final tournament of 2001. He has now retired and spends his time designing smarter bows.

freestyle

19

Office Chair Ballet

A more artistic and athletic version of synchronized chair swimming (see page 56). Guaranteed to bring out a worker's feminine side; therefore justifiable on office time as an interactive gender-awareness program.

Object >> To dance a short ballet entirely on wheeled office swivel chairs; can be classical or contemporary. Success judged by audience applause and number of hits on YouTube.

Dancers >> prima ballerina, premier danseur, two optional second leads, corps de ballet (chorus)

Stage >> a large meeting room, with desks and chairs cleared to one end, where audience sit, or any large, clearable factory floor

Equipment >>
● swivel chairs (with armrests) on wheels, one for each dancer
● sound system (either public or synchronized iPods)
● masking tape for marking performance area
● costumes to suit
● screens/dividers to make scenery

Rules >>

● audiences must synchronize their iPods or music should be played aloud

● there should be dances for the chorus, at least one pas de deux (duet), at least two solos and an ensemble finale

● ballet must include jumps and lifts

● dancers may stand, pose, or bend their bodies anyway around the chairs

● feet may be used to push off and guide

Officials >>
● choreographer
● music director
● costume designer
● videocam operator

Level of fitness >>

✓ high

☐ med

☐ low

WM stat >>

The most affecting Office Chair Ballet ever performed was the all-male Swan Lake danced in 2007 by clerical and mechanical staff (including robots) of Cheap Wheels Budget Truck Rentals of Flint, MI. It got over a million hits online.

freestyle

21

Pencil Karate

A game that can go on indefinitely and undercover; as the technique is all in the mind, people can train and prepare for this event while seemingly busy at their workstation.

Object >> To break a pencil in half, using a single karate chop. He/she who successfully breaks the pencil of everyone in the office (below boss class) receives a black belt and may be addressed as "sensei" or whatever martial arts name they adopt.

Players >> any number can play

Dojo >> any office or cubicle; can also be done in the public realm, but not the restroom, where the humidity might warp the pencils

Equipment >>
- wooden and graphite pencils (without erasers on the end)
- a focused mind
- ninja robes (optional)

Rules >>

● once you enter the game you must accept any challenge made on your pencil

● each player gets three chops on an opponent's pencil; if the pencil is not snapped, the player must allow his/her pencil to be attacked

● the game begins with single pencil attacks

● only when a player has snapped 100 pencils may they progress to snapping pencils in multiples of three; no one has even snapped more than nine pencils simultaneously

Officials >>
● sensei to inspect the pencils before and after to ensure they have not been tampered with
● feng shui master to clear inauspicious sha (optional)

Level of fitness >>

✓	high
	med
	low

WM stat >>

The record for number of pencils broken in one day is held by inventory clerk and Black Belt Frank J. Loomis (pencil name: Massive Ox) who snapped 406 standard graphite pencils in two hours in 1996 at a book depository in Pleasantville, NY.

freestyle

Office Chair Stunt Jumping

A reckless game started by the IT support team at Montana Tech, Butte, in honor of the city's daredevil son, Evel Knievel. Unless you work for a digital game designer or an extreme sport company, this event will get you fired and/or crippled, which makes it even more fun.

Object >> to ride a wheeled office chair over a ramp jumping as many obstacles/people as you can

Riders >> as many who dare; volunteers to lie in the path of the chair: as many as dare

Course >> long, flat area with open-ended ramp (taken from the warehouse or improvised) should allow space for jumper to build up speed before jump and to slow down after it

Equipment >>
● wheeled office chair, with armrests and footrests
● padded envelope knee pads and helmet
● ramp
● objects to lay behind the ramp for chair to jump over
● masking tape to mark start of jump
● measuring tape to verify length of jump
● video camera/cellphone with camera to record event

Rules >>

● riders and volunteers sign a waiver indemnifying everybody before they start

● rider must first jump the ramp without obstacles; this jump will be measured

● rider must successfully demonstrate he/she can jump the distance that will be needed to clear desired amount of objects before object jump can be attempted

● only after successfully demonstrating the ability to clear the object may the rider move on to jumping people

● fiery hoops disallowed

Officials >>
● two pushers to get the rider started
● scrutineer to measure distance and height of jump
● record keeper to log results

Level of fitness >>

✓	high
	med
	low

WM stat >>

In 2008, game tester Sonny Falco jumped 18 ft over three volunteers and four iMacs, reaching a height of 4 ft 6 ins; his chair splintered under him on landing, but he was uninjured.

freestyle

25

Ruler Fencing

Ambitious workforces hosting an entire day's medieval tournament could introduce Ruler Fencing as a supplementary game, to suit those who are not comfortable on chair back. (The bigger you make the event, the less management can do about it, especially as you will all be armed.)

Object >> to hit your opponent on the body with your epee (ruler) three times or disarm him/her to win the bout

Fencers >> teams of seven; each fencer duels with every other fencer in the seven to produce an overall winner

Equipment >>
● wooden or steel rulers padded with masking or duct tape, with the tip loaded with red marker to show where hits land
● white T shirt worn over clothes OR bib made out of white copier paper so that marks show up
● wire trash can visor helmets

Ground >> long, narrow corridor to allow fencers to stay in line; if you are playing Zorro Rules, you use the entire office, and jump on and off at least three tables during the fight

Rules >>

● fencers must kiss their rulers and honor their opponent before starting

● the bout is over if a fencer is marked by three separate hits on the torso

● best of three bouts is the winner

● when playing Zorro Rules, the bout may go on for as long as it takes for one of the fencers to declare 'I yield'

● when playing Zorro Rules, helmets may be discarded and you may write your initial on your opponent's forehead with your ruler point if the opportunity presents itself

Officials >>
● four judges to assess success of the hits
● re-inker (for the rulers)

Level of fitness >>

✓ high	
med	
low	

WM stat >>

In 2005, Ulrich Rickenbacker, an accountant from Stuttgart, recently transferred to Porsche USA in Atlanta, GA, became the first non-US born State Ruler Fencing Champion.

freestyle

Chariot Racing

Since Russell Crowe's *Gladiator*, workforce slaves have yearned to throw off the yoke of tyranny and control their own destinies. This is an exhilarating way to do it.

Object >> to race around a predetermind course without falling out of chair and pass the finish line to win

Chariot teams >> Depends on office size; you can have just two, or like the Romans, four leagues with up to ten teams in each. A team consists of one charioteer in charge of steering and speed, and two or four "horses" (people) pulling the chair.

Course >> Must be a circuit and incorporate corners and sharp turns and allow for two chariots to pass each other. Depending on your office architecture, course can be the perimeter of an office or a whole floor.

Equipment >>
● wheeled office chair, with armrests and footrests
● reins (made from string or tape) to control the horses
● padded envelope knee pads and helmet
● masking tape to mark start of course

Rules >>

● charioteers must shout out directions and desired speed to their horses

● charioteers may stand in their chairs

● races may run from three to 10 laps

● one charioteer fall per race permitted

● if a horse falls there may be one substitution

Officials >>
● starter (who also signifies end of race)
● course designer and maintenance engineer
● horse wranglers (provide water and food for horses)
● field crew (to clear accident debris from the course)

Level of fitness >>

✓	high
	med
	low

WM stat >>

Racing an *auriga* (four horses) in the Standard Life Anti-Imperial Games (2006), Max Decker blew out two front wheels, but went on to win the race.

freestyle

Elevator Tag

Very exhilarating and calls for great tactical skills. The event can be run as a covert game played among "civilians" who don't know what is going on; you may squeeze it past the board as a cheaper form of in-house incentivizing paintball.

Object >> to get around the whole building via elevators (stairs may not be used) back to finish line without being tagged

Players >> two teams, each made up of both hares and hounds; hares are the runners whose goal is to prevent the other team's hound's from tagging them out, while the hounds' goal is to eliminate the other team's hares

Course >> can only be run in a building with multiple elevators; best played where there are banks of elevators for fast changeovers to escape up or down

Equipment >>
- elevators
- rubber stamps for tagging
- identifying colors (hare or hound)
- masking tape to mark agreed finish line

Rules >>

● freight elevators may be used

● when a hare is rubber stamped, he /she is out of the game and must report to the course referee

● last hare standing is the winner

● the race shall be over when last hare is tagged, or the office day officially ends, whichever comes first

Officials >>
● starter
● course referees
● course designer

Level of fitness >>

☐	high
✓	med
☐	low

WM stat >>

This game was invented in 1962 by Madison Avenue account executive J. Walter Beemster, fleeing from a posse of enraged clients.

freestyle

Staple Gun Quickdraw

Great indoor game, and allows the non-jocks to shine. The players must start as soon as the whistle blows. The judges' decision is final, but there is a People's Prize for the one that the workforce liked the best (decided by vote).

Object >> to create the most artistic work-related image with a stapler in two minutes

Players >> two artists play against each other in any one contest; there can be as many contests played as necessary/desired

Canvas >> two sheets of 8 ½ ins x 11 ins paper stuck to a wall-mounted corkboard

Equipment >>
● staple guns and supply of staples
● 8 ½ ins x 11 ins paper
● corkboards
● list of random work-related subjects gathered from a secret ballot of the nonstapling workforce (e.g., company logo, boss's car, the chairman, etc.)

Rules >>

● staplers must be in shoot mode (opened out flat)

● no staple must be shot before the start signal

● if stapler jams, the artist must change to a new one

● artists shall cease stapling and hold staplers aloft on the stop command

● artists are allowed unlimited refills

Officials >>
● starter/finisher
● staple caddies
● four judges

Level of fitness >>

	high
	med
✓	low

WM stat >>

Wesley B. Creswell's Warhol-esque Multiple Logo (he worked for IBM), created in 2000, was bought by MoMA, New York, for an undisclosed sum.

freestyle

33

Office Chair Rowing: Coxed Eight

This is a classic event established in the mid 1990s. Few managers would dare ban it because the event is now part of the Fringe Team Building movement, and they would look foolish and removed from Modern Management Methods. If space permits, races can include up to four teams of eight. The event is central to any Office Regatta.

Object >> to row as fast as possible from one end of your office space to the other

Rowers >> eight rowers and one cox. Teams can be mixed male and female, and each team is allowed up to three imported rowers from other office departments

Course >> 50 yds in a straight line, although course may be adapted to local conditions

Equipment >>
Per crew:
● nine wheeled office chairs (the front one facing the other eight)
● strong rubber bands or plastic packaging tape to hold chairs together

● masking tape for start and finish line
● stopwatch or cellphone with stopwatch function

Rules >>

● eights must row from one end of the office to the other while using imaginary rowing technique with the upper body and skill of footwork for propulsion

● ramming will result in disqualification

● time points awarded for style

Officials >>
● course designer
● two umpires
● starter

Level of fitness >>

✓	high
	med
	low

WM stat >>

The fastest time ever recorded is 49.9 seconds by the IT support team of the NASA Jet Propulsion Lab in May 1999.

water sports

Office Chair Rowing: Single Scull Time Trials

An adaptable solo event, this can be raced in both large global megacorps or small businesses as well. Set up an interdepartmental league, culminating in a mano a mano with each department's scullmeister. When you have an overall champion, challenge rival companies.

Object >> to be the fastest rower over a predetermined distance

Rowers >> minimum two*, no official maximum

* freelancers can compete solo in their home office, racing against their best times, but must appoint an external arbitrator to verify result to qualify for inclusion in the league

Course >> Must be a straight line, but length can vary according to environment. Lanes must be clearly marked.

Equipment >>
● one wheeled office chair per competitor
● masking tape to mark start and finish lines, and lanes
● stopwatch, or cellphone with stopwatch function

Rules >>

● scullers must use consistent rowing motion with arms as they propel themselves with their footwork

● chairs must be of uniform size and weight; the lightweight German designed Buro "Freisitz," with armrests stripped off, is the preferred model

● drug testing may be implemented if the referees suspect caffeine abuse

● colleagues may not give the chair a push to gain unfair momentum

Officials >>
● timekeeper/starter
● two umpires
● independent invigilator (see Rowers opposite page)

Level of fitness >>

✓ high
☐ med
☐ low

WM stat >>

The still unbeaten star of single sculling is B. Lennox Poindexter, a Yale intern from Young & Rubicam who covered 40 yds in 35.02 seconds at the 1987 Madison Avenue regatta.

water sports

Office Chair Rowing: Coxless Pairs

This is a two-person event and can only be played in companies where staff levels allow enough compatible pairs to be made up. Makes an exciting event in any regatta program.

Object >> race as pairs over fixed distance, using only arms and legs; first over the line wins

Rowers >> two teams, minimum of four players; no more than four teams

Course >> you will need an unencumbered corridor or passage at least 50 yds long; can have a slight curve but not sharp bends.

Equipment >>
Per crew:

● per pair, two office chairs lashed together with duct tape or plastic duct tape in line OR a standard dimension mail cart with room for two to sit in line

● masking tape for start and finish line

Rules >>

● no more than four pairs in any one race

● rowers should be of same weight within a 2-lb tolerance; if one pair is lighter they should carry extra ballast in the form of date-sensitive memos from the HR department

● while using imaginary rowing technique with the upper body rowers must use footwork for propulsion

● kicking, shoving, or interference will be penalized by disqualification

● jokes and innuendoes about pairs, if overheard by a referee, incur a five second penalty

Officials >>
● timekeeper/starter
● head referee and assistant referees, one stationed every 10 yds

Level of fitness >>

✓ high	
☐ med	
☐ low	

WM stat >>

The current record (65 yds in 40 seconds, while simultaneously losing the company $1 million per second on the overnight yen market) is held by a pair of foreign trade speculators from Lehmann Brothers.

water sports

Office Chair Kayak Slalom

This event requires a long, steep incline for maximum efficiency. Ideal for offices with sloped corridors or ramped parking garages. Competitors must race one at a time, and their runs are timed; it is fast and furious and probably not suitable for a workforce made up of employees over the age of 35.

Object >> to make your way down a sloped course weaving in and out of obstacles without touching them; fastest time with least obstacles touched wins

Canoeists>> unlimited

Course >> Corridor or passageway between 50 yds and 100 yds long that turns at least one 90 degree corner and slopes down or uphill (no more than I in 3); must contain between 20 and 30 hazards laid out. Obstacles should include trashcans, small filing cabinets, watercooler refills and piles of copier paper.

Equipment >>
● one office chair per person
● paddle of choice
● hardhat
● obstacles
● masking tape for start and finish line
● stopwatch or cellphone with stopwatch function

Rules >>

● hardhats must be worn

● competitor must go round all obstacles; if a hazard is knocked over or out of place, competitor must return to the start

● if competitors capsize, they may get back on the chair and start again from the capsize spot, designated by the nearest referee

● colleagues may not give the chair a push to gain unfair momentum

Officials >>
● timekeeper/starter
● two–10 referees (depending on course length)
● qualified first aid providers

Level of fitness >>

✓	high
	med
	low

WM stat >>

In 2001, Butler Wivenhoe III, whizzkid CEO of Buttkiss.com, spun too fast into an early turn and hit all 27 obstacles, making an all time-slowest record of 3:30 minutes over a 100-yard course.

water sports

Desktop Surfing

Very popular on the West Coast, so it's no surprise that Silicon Valley fields the most champions. This event tests balance and coolness under pressure. It can be a solo time trial or a Big Ride for as many surfers as will fit in the office.

Object >> To stay upright on a desk using classic surfer maneuvers, while teams of colleagues try to unbalance you by pulling and shaking the desks you are standing on. Last dude standing is the winner.

Surfers >> unlimited

Course >> Two standard desks positioned in parallel, with a gap of 10 ins between them; course can be set up in an open plan space or a traditional office.

Equipment >>
Per crew:
● two office desks
● two Wavemaker teams of robust colleagues to shift desks
● sound system (optional: players may wear iPods but play synchronized tunes on a pre-agreed shuffle)

Rules >>

● desks are to be shaken, not moved around

● three wipeouts allowed per competitor; after that, surfer is disqualified

● no wavemaker team may comprise more than 4 slackers

● no polishing/or other tampering of the desks before the competition

● advanced players may elect to ride desks of different heights

Officials >>
● wave manager
● lifeguard

Level of fitness >>

✓	high
	med
	low

WM stat >>

The awesomest all-round desk surfing dude is in fact a dudette—California software dreamgirl Ms. Thursday Peralta, who rode her desks for one whole shift (July 7, 2007), while hosting an international video conference call with the Tokyo office.

water sports

White Water Stairway Rafting

Adrenaline-rich extreme office sport that can be combined with Elevator Tag (see page 30) for maximum excitement and the possibility of work slowdown injury time. Some actual rafting experience useful here. It is a long event, as competitors have to build their own rafts; some organizers like to offer a prize for Best Raft as a secondary incentive.

Object >> To build a serviceable raft and take it down your building's stairs. Course can be as long or short as you like but must end in the lobby. Most stairways will only accommodate two rafts at a time, but rafts can be set off at staggered intervals (decided on by handicapping for previous speeds, age, experience, etc.) by the Raft Marshal. The focus then moves to who can overtake whom on the landings.

Rafters >> this can be a solo event or raced between teams of two, three, or four persons

Equipment >>
Per crew:
● supply of robust cardboard packaging, duct tape, etc. for raft building
● cardboard tube rafting poles
● stairwell containing at least three flights of stairs

Rules >>

● safety regulations demand that all rafters must be able to walk up and down one flight of stairs fully clothed and carrying a laptop

● raft should be built from scratch

● all rafts must be certified by the Raft Safety Officer before launch

● overshooting into the basement means automatic disqualification

● rafters must stay in raft while negotiating turns

● teams may make temporary repairs while on the move

Officials >>
● raft Marshal
● raft Safety Officer
● stair guards (one on each flight)

Level of fitness >>

✓	high
	med
	low

WM stat >>

In 2008, a team from Colorado Mutual shot the stairway of the 56-storey Republic Plaza in Denver in 25 minutes, but lost a man on the treacherous final run into the three-storey marble lobby.

water sports

Swivel Chair Swim Race Medley

A more inclusive event in which competitors can choose their own style. Can form part of a Swimming Gala and is a popular choice for interdepartmental or intercompany competitions. Keen ones can work out a program of eliminatory heats to include everyone in the office.

Object >> To swim a wheeled swivel chair over the equivalent of an Olympic-sized pool by laying across it on your front and moving arms and legs in your chosen style. Course can be two, four, or six lengths. First one to swim from one end of the pool to the other, then back, back wins.

Swimmers >> between four and eight swimmers per heat

Course >> Ideally, space equivalent to Olympic size pool (164 ft x82 ft) divided into 10 lanes, of which the inner eight may be used and should be 8 ft 2 ins wide. This may have to be the parking lot. There must be a wall, or temporary barrier at the end of 82 ft length. Improvise.

Equipment >>
● swivel chairs (armrests removed) on wheels, one for each swimmer
● masking tape to mark lanes
● a bell or buzzer for the winner to ring when they get back to the start line

Rules >>

● the race starts when the starter whistle is blown and swimmers dash from their desks to their chairs, which are in position

● swimmers may use their feet and hands to kick off/push off from start of course and off back wall

● swimmers may use their hands and feet to push off the ground but must maintain swimming-stroke motions while they propel themselves

● swimmers must touch the wall/barrier at the end of a length

● swimmers may use any style of swimming they choose except backstroke

● swimmers must ring bell/buzzer when they complete the race

Officials >>
● starter/timekeeper
● lifeguard (one at end of each lane)

Level of fitness >>

	high
✓	med
	low

WM stat >>

Surprisingly, the record for the fastest freestyle swim over two lengths (38 seconds, 2000) remains with Otis Johansson, a dry goods importer from Omaha, Nebraska.

water sports

Swivel Chair Relay Race

Another one for the Swimming Gala program; each department can field their own relay team. The changeover is pivotal.

Object >> Four or six swimmers each to swim a wheeled swivel chair (as in Swivel Chair Swim Medley) over an Olympic length, handing the baton over at the end of each length. First one back wins.

Swimmers >> between four and eight teams of four to six swimmers

Equipment >>
● swivel chairs (armrests removed) on wheels, one for each swimmer
● masking tape to mark lanes
● a bell or buzzer for the winner to ring when they get back to the start line
● baton

Course >> Ideally, space equivalent to Olympic size pool (164 ft x82 ft) divided into 10 lanes, of which the inner eight may be used and should be 8 ft 2 ins wide. This may have to be the parking lot. There must be a wall, or temporary barrier at the end of 82 ft length. Improvise.

Rules >>

● the race starts when the starter whistle is blown and swimmers dash from their desks to their chairs, which are in position

● swimmers may use their feet and hands to kick off/push from the start

● swimmers may use their hands and feet to push off the ground but must maintain swimming-stroke motions

● if the baton is dropped, the swimmer must pick it up without getting off the chair, leaving their lane or ramming other swimmers

Officials >>
● starter/timekeeper
● lifeguard (one at end of each lane)
● first aid provider

Level of fitness >>

✓	high
	med
	low

WM stat >>

A relay team from the Dade County Police Records Dept. were disqualified and stripped of their Golden Mousemats for indiscriminate ramming and baton tampering during the notoriously bad-tempered 2000 state finals in Florida.

water sports

Swivel Chair Backstroke

A third event suitable for a Swimming Gala. Swimmers lie on their backs over the chairs and propel themselves along using backstroke movements with the arms and kicking with legs. Organizers are advised to have swimmers sign a waiver exonerating them from any culpability in case of crippling back damage.

Object >> to swim a wheeled swivel chair (as in Swivel Chair Swim Medley) over an Olympic length (82ft) using only backstroke

Swimmers >> between four and eight

Course >> Ideally, space equivalent to Olympic size pool (164 ft x 82 ft) divided into 10 lanes, of which the inner eight may be used and should be 8 ft 2 ins wide. This may have to be the parking lot. There must be a wall, or temporary barrier at the end of 82 ft length. Improvise.

Equipment >>
● swivel chairs (armrests removed) on wheels, one for each swimmer
● masking tape to mark lanes
● a bell or buzzer for the winner to ring when they get back to the start line

Rules >>

● the race starts when the starter whistle is blown and swimmers dash from their desks to their chairs, which are in position

● swimmers may use their feet and hands to kick off/push off from start

● swimmers may use their hands and feet to push off the ground but must maintain swimming-stroke motions

● swimmers must use backstroke ONLY

Officials >>
● starter/timekeeper/baton scrutineer
● lifeguard (one at end of each lane)
● first aid provider

Level of fitness >>

✓	high
☐	med
☐	low

WM stat >>

The US record (1 minute 12 seconds) was smashed in 2009 by an Australian Visiting Professor at Michigan State University, who swam the length in 55 seconds, just before giving her paper on Dolphin Flipper Dynamics.

water sports

Cubicle Diving 1

This extreme event is inspired by the fad for sealing off a vacationing coworker's cubicle and filling it with either packing peanuts, paper cups, torn out magazine pages, or shredded confidential documentation. The cubicle must be emptied of office equipment first. Divers do so at their own risk and should sign a waiver to that effect.

Object >> To dive from atop a desk into a cubicle full of packing peanuts, executing a graceful maneuver on the way. The diver who gets the highest marks out of ten wins.

Drivers >> maximum six; if more wish to compete, split the contest into two heats

Diving Board >> a standard desk, cleared of objects, pushed up against the cubicle wall, and two planks placed between desk and floor, to allow diver a run up if required.

Equipment >>
- duct tape to seal up the cubicle
- enough packing peanuts to cushion the landing of an average person (between 120 and 180 lbs in weight)
- a height gauge
- cellphone with video function (for instant replays)

Rules >>

● diver may take a run from a distance or go from a standing start on the desk

● diver must announce their intended dive (tuck, pike, half somersault, pancake, feet first, fetal position, etc.) BEFORE the dive

● extra points will be awarded for lift and height

● diver is judged on best of three dives

Officials >>
● starter
● lifeguard
● packing peanut replenisher
● panel of four judges who will mark on style, technique, enthusiasm and smoothness of entry into packing peanuts

Level of fitness >>

	high
✓	med
	low

WM stat >>

The highest dive (12 ft at the height of its arc), incorporating a tuck and half somersault was achieved in New York in 2009 by UN interpreter Arkady Mishkin, who later turned professional.

water sports

Cubicle Diving 2

A variation on Cubicle Diving 1; the extra height allows divers to demonstrate a wider variety of styles.

Object >> To dive from a chair on a desk into a cubicle full of packing peanuts, executing a graceful maneuver on the way. The diver who gets the highest marks out of ten wins.

Divers >> maximum six; if more wish to compete, split the contest into two heats

Equipment >>
● duct tape to seal up the cubicle
● enough packing peanuts to cushion the landing of an average person (between 120 and 180 54lbs in weight)
● a height gauge
● cellphone with video function (for instant replays)
● a standard fixed-leg chair

Diving Board >> a standard desk, cleared of objects, pushed up against the cubicle wall, and two planks placed between desk and floor, to allow diver a running start if required, and a fixed leg chair mounted securely on the desktop; extra height can be achieved by lashing filled box files to the chair seat.

Rules >>

● diver must announce their intended dive (half somersault, pancake, feet first, fetal position, etc.) BEFORE the dive

● extra points will be awarded for height of dive

Officials >>
● starter
● lifeguard
● packing peanuts replenisher
● panel of four judges who will mark on style, technique, enthusiasm, and smoothness of packing peanut entry

Level of fitness >>

☐ high	
☑ med	
☐ low	

WM stat >>

In January 2010 an entire acoustic ceiling was brought down as a result of an over-enthusiastic open pike by Walter MacAloon, in the administration department of a North Virginia correctional facility.

water sports

Synchronized Chair Swimming

A more restful event which can be performed by most age groups and abilities, and can be escalated into a cross departmental competition or retained as an entertainment display between swim races. You will need lots of rehearsal time, which will also encourage office romance, both excellent for slowing down the work process.

Object >> to be part of a choreographed set of swimming movements interpreting a story, mood, or song to suit your workplace. Consider "Working in a Coal Mine," Parton's "9–5," Dylan's "Maggie's Farm," Campbell's "Wichita Lineman."

Swimmers >> no fewer than six, otherwise synchronicity does not work; teams can be mixed or single gender

Equipment >>
● swivel chairs (with armrests) on wheels; swimmers are responsible for the maintenance and regular oiling of their own wheels
● sound system (either public or synchronized iPods)

Course >> any large empty space that allows gliding and Busby Berkeley-style formations; the lobby is ideal as then spectators can watch from gallery height and catch the full beauty of the display

Rules >>

● the display starts on the choreographer's signal. Judges should be provided with iPods if the music source is not public

● swimmers should display graceful competence in arm movements, leg moments, gliding between each other without collisions, and smiling at all times

● swimmers should all stop together; staggered stopping will accrue penalty points

● extra marks will be given for creative use of limbs

Officials >>
● choreographer
● dj
● team of four judges to award points on concept, style, technique, and execution

Level of fitness >>

	high	
✓	med	
	low	

WM stat >>

The IRS Ladies Synchronized Swimming team's signature routine (Show Me the Money) has consistently won top place in the last three WM polls, and they are three time winners of their own industry's top honor, the Capone.

water sports

Competitive Fishing

A sedentary event that will favor experience and guile over youth and beauty. It can safely be played during consciousness-raising meetings, budget discussions, or quarterly assessments. For shorter games, play Blackjack (first to get to 21) or first to 100.

Object >> To take turns fishing business cards (the fish) out of the trashcan with an office-made rod; each card is assigned a score and whoever gets the highest score wins (and may be photographed with his highest scoring card).

Anglers >> two minimum, 10 maximum

Course >> Can take place anywhere, but the trashcan must be correctly stocked. There should be only one CEO card but increasing numbers of lower ranks. - Harvard Business School Rules prescribe a minimum of 25 Sales Manager cards

Equipment >>
● trashcan (empty)
● packing peanuts
● business cards of the higher management, with small string loops attached, and each given a mark out of 100
● fishing rods (assembled from pencils or ballpoints, string and paperclips)
● scorecard

Rules >>

● anglers must make their own fishing rods, hooks and bait out of standard office equipment

● anglers take turns to fish (by name, in alphabetical order). As soon as a fish is caught, it is the next angler's turn, and so on until all fish are caught

● anglers keep their fish and must be prepared to show them to the umpire whenever requested

● any pilfering of a competitor's catch are grounds for immediate disqualification

● exaggeration of your catch, while not illegal, is considered bad form

Officials >>
● scorechecker
● umpire

Level of fitness >>

☐ high	
☐ med	
✓ low	

WM stat >>

A round of competitive fishing started at the Nantucket-based Ishmael & Melville Loss Adjusters in 1998 is still going on; two competitors had to withdraw from the competition when they retired.

water sports

Watercooler Relay Dash

An old favorite first played in the US in the 1970s. Popular in UK since the tea trolley was replaced by on-site watercoolers.

. . . .

Object >> To run a course of ten watercoolers, stopping at each one to drink a paper cup of water. First one home is the winner, subsequent runners place second, third, and fourth respectively.

Field >> minimum of 10 runners

Course >> May be a clear, flat surface or desk hurdles may be introduced. Vertical course may also be used where the watercoolers are on different floors in the building, but runners may not use elevators.

Equipment >>
● 10 watercooler stations.
● a short version can be played with 5 watercoolers
● paper cups

Rules >>

● paper cups must be filled by runner

● paper cups must be drained before runner can resume his/her run

● pushing or tripping opponents results in instant disqualification

● paper cups must be filled to the brim

Officials >>
● umpire at each cooler
● starter

Level of fitness >>

✓	high
	med
	low

WM stat >>

The world's most gruelling watercooler relay is run over a vertical course of 10 floors in the John Hancock Building, Chicago, Illinois.

track and field

61

Partition Hurdles

Hi-energy event much in vogue with the young IT crowd and paralegals who want to let out their inner jock. Can be run as a departmental competition or inter-departmental event.

Object >> To clear a course of 16 workstation partitions without knocking any down or falling over, in the fastest possible time. First across the finish line wins.

Field >> four to six runners per race

Course >> A long straight run with at least 4 ft between desks. Runners run up to the first desk, jump on it, hurdle the partition to the adjacent desk, jump down, take a pace and jump up to next desk and so on.

Equipment >>
● 16 workstations in which two desks sandwich a partition screen no more than 5 ft high. Desks must be cleared of all equipment.
● finish flag
● stopwatch or cellphone with stop watch function

Rules >>

● hurdles must be cleared completely

● runners must stay in their lane

● spiked shoes may not be worn

● if you fall, you must get up again within 10 seconds

● false starts will be penalized with time points

Officials >>
● starter
● finishing line judges

Level of fitness >>

✓	high
	med
	low

WM stat >>

In the late 1980s Russian cosmonauts trained for weightless administration on partition hurdles in a zero gravity facility in Kazakhstan.

track and field

Downstairs Running

An old-school event that remains popular because it requires very little equipment or specialist skill and can be set up and dismantled without management's knowledge.

Object >> to race down stairs from the top of the building to the bottom in the quickest possible time

Field >> four plus; in some states health & safety rules apply, depending on width and angle of staircase

Course >> Descent of at least four flights of stairs; if racing in a very tall building, course may be a section of the full staircase; there must be an elevator to take the runners up to the starting point. The finish line must be clearly defined.

Equipment >>
● cellphones for all participants; news of the event is announced minutes before the start, like a flash mob event
● stair marshals (one per flight)

Rules >>

● runners may compete solo or as part of a peloton (the bunched formation favored by Tour de France cyclists races, which saves energy, allows slipstreaming and cuts down drag), in which case they must wear identification bands

● bumping into your opponents incurs disqualification and a total season ban

● jumping over the banister (if present) results in disqualification

Officials >>
● starter/timekeeper
● stair marshals (one per flight)
● waterboys

Level of fitness >>

☐ high	
✓ med	
☐ low	

WM stat >>

The largest field (502 runners) in this event turned out in 2005 for the race down four sets of stairs (one on each corner) of the Seagram Building in New York, won by a peloton of busboys from the Four Seasons restaurant.

track and field

Office Chair Solo Sprint

A simple one-on-one race over a short distance that is suitable for medium and small offices. If performed properly, it can make you look ultra eager to get to your workstation.

Object >> to cover a short distance (25 yds maximum) as fast as possible using only an office chair and your feet

Field >> two to six runners, depending on the size of the course

Course >> A short, flat indoor or outdoor course with no obstacles. Can be run on the parking lot after working hours, but that would be on your own time so would not count in any workplace league.

Equipment >>
● wheeled office chair, armrests removed. Sprinters may further strip down the chair if they wish.
● masking tape to mark start and finish lines
● cellphone with camera for photo finishes

Rules >>

● arms may be used to help propulsion

● at their own risk, sprinters may start by spinning the chair to gain momentum

● runners must stay seated but can lean in any direction to build up speed

● the entire chair wheelbase and all the sprinter's limbs must be over the finish line to win

Officials >>
● starter/ timekeeper
● finish line judge

Level of fitness >>

	high	☐
✓	med	
	low	

WM stat >>

The world record chair sprint (7.998 seconds) was set by Ricky Copper in 2004 at General Motors Head Office, Detroit, Michigan. Allegations of a secret remote-controlled booster engine in his chair have never been proven.

track and field

Frisbee Trials

An indoor version of an outdoor favorite. Can be played from the comfort of your desk.

Object >> to demonstrate best overall skills with a frisbee (a CD) in three mini events: Distance Throwing (farthest throw wins); Freestyle (throwing and catching frisbee in as many different ways as possible); Doggy Fashion (catcher rises to the thrown fisbee and catches it between his/her teeth)

Slackers >> two plus, but always in teams of two

Equipment >>
● old CDs from account archive
● numbered labels for marking where they land

Course >> the trials adapt to fit into any available space and may be all seated (union) or all free running (league) but not a mixture of both.

Rules >>

● only discs from officially authorized archive sources may be used

● discs must not be weighted at the rim or tampered with in any way

● competitors must play all three games to qualify

● in distance trials, final mark is best of three

● in Doggy Fashion final mark is best of five

Officials >>
● frisbee wrangler to measure distance of throw
● timer/referee
● panel of two judges who will award points for style, form and accuracy

Level of fitness >>

□ high	
✓ med	
□ low	

WM stat >>

White House aides in the Bush II administration were consistently trashed by the formidable team of Barney and Spot Bush with their human thrower (allowable under subsidiary rule 404/c). Bo Obama has yet to play.

track and field

Toner Cartridge Shot Put

Inpired by Highland Games, and the shot put, this is an exciting and dangerous game, a rare opportunity for the tech support serf with good upper arm strength to shine. It also solves the problem of what to do with old toner cartridges.

Object >> athlete who throws the cartridge the farthest distance wins

Object >> unlimited; there is a Men's and Women's class

Course >> large window-free area cleared of breakables with a central spot (6 in diameter) where the thrower stands, and concentric circles marked at 10 ft (white), 15 ft (green), 20 ft (yellow), 25 ft (blue), and 30 ft (red)

Equipment >>
● wheeled office chair (optional)
● tape measure (digital, electronic or standard dressmaker)
● white, yellow, green, blue, and red chalk or masking tape to mark the throwing circles
● supply of used toner cartridges

Rules >>

● the cartridges must be empty; this is the contender's responsibility

● shot-putters may stand and turn (on spot) OR spin on spot in swivel chair to build up centripetal force

● cartridge must leave hand after three spins

● spectators must stand beyond the largest circle

Officials >>
● starter/ timekeeper
● two distance measurers
● first aid team

Level of fitness >>

✓	high		
	med		
	low		

WM stat >>

This event was accidentally invented by enraged secretary Velma M. Ducati of Arkansas Electronic Solutions, who hurled a cartridge out of the window after an incident involving streaked pages. She still holds the Woman's Distance record (98 ft).

track and field

Middle Distance Coffee Run

An all-weather event for junior staff only, usually run mid-morning and mid-afternoon, depending on the level of caffeine addiction in the officers of the board.

Object >> Contenders must go to a coffee shop and buy six coffees (minimum) of various kinds specified by senior staff, then return to the office without spilling any and distributing the coffee correctly. First one to make it back and successfully distribute the coffees is the winner.

Contenders >> 2-6 (gender immaterial)

Equipment >>
● one cardboard coffee tray per competitor

Course >> Variable. It can be the nearest coffee shop, which is good for novices; but if you are running uppity interns, or overambitious assistant managers, challenge them by designating the nearest non-Starbucks.

Rules >>

● coffee getters must memorize the order

● coffee must still be drinkable on return

● coffee getters must not call in their order ahead

● coffee getters must not drink the coffee or buy any for themselves

Officials >>
● starter/ timekeeper
● caffeine auditor (to make sure each order is correctly fulfilled)

Level of fitness >>

	high	
✓	med	
	low	

WM stat >>

The most coffees ever correctly purchased in the shortest time was 12, in a round trip of only 6 minutes, by US Navy SEAL Jack Tarr on secret assignment to a classified arms company in Seattle in 2004.

track and field

Office Chair Derby

Inspired by the Kentucky Derby run at Churchill Downs; runners sit back to front on their office chairs, jockey style. The Kentucky is open to 3-year-old colts and fillies, so this is an event for anyone in their third year at the workplace.

Object >> to race over an oval course; first chair and rider past the post wins, second, third, fourth, and fifth place respectively.

Riders >> full field of 20

Course >> Churchill Downs , where the Kentucky is run, is 1 ¼ miles long (10 furlongs) in the shape of a horizontally squashed donut. An open plan office where an oval course can be laid out round the cubicles, allowing spectators to stay in the center is ideal.

Equipment >>
● wheeled office chair armrests removed
● masking tape to mark start and finish lines
● cellphone with camera for photo finishes
● optional cruelty-free whip (made from ruler and rubber bands looped together to form a knotted chain)

Rules >>

● feet must be used to gallop

● riders must wear silks of choice

● chair must be named

● riders may hold on to chairback

● riders may stand up in the saddle

Officials >>
● starter/ timekeeper
● referees
● pit stop crew

Level of fitness >>

✓	high
☐	med
☐	low

WM stat >>

In 1999, attempts at corporate law firm Weltschmerz Macarthur to re-create Churchill Downs by sprinkling dirt on the mezzanine floor where the course was laid out resulted in rider Wesley Witherspoon being thrown. His chair broke a leg and had to be shot. Witherspoon later tested positive for Red Bull.™

track and field

Bubble Wrap Popping Challenge

The elevation of a guilty pleasure into a respectable sport, this can be played by anyone and is an excellent way to pass the last hour of Friday afternoon. There are two classes of competition, Big Bubble and Little Bubble, and they should not be used within the same game. Any technique can be used—popping by row, in circles or at random.

Object >> to get all bubbles on a regulations sheet of bubble wrap popped in the fastest time

Contenders >> unlimited; the whole department can play at once if necessary; an excellent international game as there are no language problems.

Course >> no course necessary; this can be done at the desk or in a meeting you know will be quite noisy

Equipment >>
● sheets of big bubble wrap (2 ft x 2 ft)
● sheets of small bubble wrap (1ft x 1ft)

Rules >>

● all bubbles to be popped using manual digits only

● NO stomping on bubble wrap

● excessive orgasmic shouting will be penalized with a time penalty

● contenders who work in shipping, gift wrapping or related packaging industries will carry a time handicap

● contenders must have a bubble checker with them at all times to prevent cheating

Officials >>
● starter/ timekeeper
● bubble checker

Level of fitness >>

	high
	med
✓	low

WM stat >>

The record (1,000 Large Bubbles popped in 8 mins 18.03 seconds) was set in 1997 by southpaw Viggo Viggosen, a Minnesota postal worker. He retired unbeaten two years later with an inoperable case of Bubble Thumb.

track and field

Steeplechase

Like the Derby, but a lot wilder; can be played across entire departments and with other companies on other floors.

Object >> to navigate a course of obstacles that has a series of marked points along the way. Each point has tokens (post-it notes), the riders are required to pick up. The winner is the first rider to make it through with all the tokens.

Riders >> minimum four, maximum 20

Course >> this at the course designer's discretion, but should include four hazards (90 degree turn, water jump, change of level) and at least six (maximum 10) steeples. The course can go up or downstairs via elevators but riders must not dismount

Equipment >>
● wheeled office chair, armrests removed
● masking tape to mark start and finish lines as well as directions
● cellphone with camera for photo finishes
● "steeples" made from A3 copier paper and numbered

● tokens (drawings on post-it notes will do if there are no funds) to be collected at each steeple

Rules >>

● whips may be used in moderation to fend off others

● the tokens must be collected in numerical order

● all steeples to be manned by umpires to prevent cheating. If challenged by umpires, offending rider must create a feasible explanation, the best one gets a prize

● riders must not dismount but can remount if they fall

Officials >>
● starter/ timekeeper
● course designer
● steeple point umpires

Level of fitness >>

☑ high
☐ med
☐ low

WM stat >>

Steeplechase was banned in California for a decade (1984–1994) when feng shui masters ruled that more than fivet pointed steeples in any one space opened the gates to excess malevolent sha.

track and field

BS Marathon

This is a cerebral race and so opens the field to work colleagues uncomfortable with physical challenges.

Object >> Each player is assigned a predetermined corporate-speak term that they must insert into conversation 26 times in one office day. If target is not reached, the game is carried over to the next working day.

Players >> open field; as many as want to

Course >> there is no set course but experienced players know that by hanging around the executive restroom, the VP's designated elevator, or the boardroom they can up their score very quickly.

Equipment >>
● no special equipment needed, although competitors allowed a click counter to keep track of their corporate-speak tally

Rules >>

● phrase must be in proper conversation

● e-mails, letters, faxes or text messages invalid

● extra points if introduced into a conference call

● if the phrase is repeated to a player within two hours of its launch, that player will earn an advantage of 3 (that means they can complete the race with 23 uses.) If the term is used by top management, the advantage is doubled

Officials >>
● starter/ timekeeper
● phrase assigner
● secret judges

Level of fitness >>

☐ high	
☐ med	
✓ low	

WM stat >>

The quickest-ever marathon was won in 1998, when K.T. Smith introduced the phrase at an AGM of brand strategist multinational Kumquat Boulevard and all ten creative directors repeated it back to her at once; cumulative advantage gave her the race in 1 minute 49 seconds.

track and field

Boardroom Long Jump

This is a risky physical game very popular among the arbitrage community. Many of them prefer the extreme version wherein the athletes perform their jumps on top of the table.

Object >> always played in the boardroom for symbolic purposes, this is your basic long jump competition, farthest jump wins

Jumpers >> unlimited, although you will be constrained by time

Course >> alongside the boardroom with the table and chairs moved to one side to give jumpers ample room and a single start line marked in tape

Equipment >>
● access to boardroom
● sand to scatter for grip
● tape measure
● masking tape to mark start line
● small balls of gum, pushpins or any other agreed token to mark your jump length

Rules >>

● feet must not step over the start line

● jumper must take off with both feet

● measure of jump will be where feet first landed

● each jumper must place their token at the point where they landed

Officials >>
● starter/ timekeeper
● length measurer

Level of fitness >>

✓ high	
med	
low	

WM stat >>

The longest jump ever made was in 1929 at the New York Stock Exchange at 11 Wall Street; an anonymous competitor attempted the jump on top of the highly polished table and continued out through the window.

track and field

Office Pentathlon

Borrowed from the olympic games, this could be upgraded by a clever employee slightly subversive in-office procrastination strategy to a full on team-building program, with you in charge.

Object >> Competitors must choose five events from this book (one from each of four sections and one free choice). Whoever accumulates most points over the five events wins.

Competitors >> six as solo players; you may also field teams of up to four, for joint effort. Each team member takes on one or more of the events, playing to their strengths.

Equipment >>
● as listed for the chosen games

Course >> you can either have a designated all-purpose course (usually possible in West Coast companies, where there are corporate play areas) or competitors can travel to various suitable venues around the building

Rules >>

- events must be agreed beforehand

- rules of all games must be obeyed

Officials >>
- starter/ timekeeper
- marshals
- referees

Level of fitness >>

✓	high
	med
	low

WM stat >>

This has never been played before, so any data from pentathlon events will be gratefully received by our editorial team and incorporated into the next issue.

track and field

Wastebasket Ball

A classic played in every office since as long as anyone can remember. Also played at school and college level.

Object >> to score more baskets in two sets of 15- minute halves than your opponents

Players >> two teams of 5 slackers each, with substitutes

Court>> Standard size office or large cubicle, with baskets placed at each end. Can be floor-based or partition-mounted.

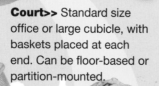

Equipment >>
● two wastepaper baskets
● waste paper
● rubber bands

Rules >>

● each team must make their own ball out of wastepaper and elastic bands

● slackers must not hold the ball for longer than 3 seconds before passing

● no running with the ball

● no standing on desks or chairs

Officials >>
● referee

Level of fitness >>

	high	
✓	med	
	low	

WM stat >>

The most successful wastebasket ball team of all time is the legendary IBM Staplers (1977 season), who netted 109 baskets in one game.

ball games

Workplace Soccer

Adaptation of the world's most popular sport, played in offices around the globe. You can field a full team (11 players) or five-a-side, and can be played sitting down or free running. If there are enough teams, you can split into leagues.

Object >> to score more goals than your opposing team while defending your own goal

Players>> Two teams of 11 (or five) players each, with three subs to be brought on in case of injury. If played sitting down you must adopt a formation (4-4-2, 5-3-2) and stay with it for the game. The goalkeeper remains in front of the goal.

Field >> Standard size office, with goals placed at each end. Can be smaller for five-a-side.

Equipment >>
● two goals (can be marked by two filing cabinets, or two items of clothing, preferably including the boss's inappropriate Armani bomber jacket)
● ball made out of waste paper and rubber bands

Rules >>

● if sitting, or standing at desk, hands must be used to "kick" instead of feet; no throwing allowed

● if free running, ball must not touch hand or arm (unless you are goalkeeper)

● players must determine an offside rule and stick to it

● any player called away from the game for work purposes is deemed injured, and a sub may be brought on

Officials >>
● referee
● four referee's assistants
● first aid provider

Level of fitness >>

	high
✓	med
	low

WM stat >>

Arguments still rage about the 1986 match between Bank of Argentina Ladies and the visiting fact-finding team from the Bank of England, in which a controversial hand ball won the game for Argentina.

ball games

Cubicle Tennis

Another classic, popular with all workforces since the introduction of cubicle walls in the late 1950s. Both singles and doubles versions can be played.

Object >> to hit the ball to each other over the partition without it touching the partition or going out of play; scoring is the same as for standard tennis

Players >> two same sex; four same sex or four mixed sex

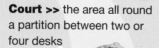

Court >> the area all round a partition between two or four desks

Equipment >>
● balls made from rubber bands (players make their own)
● raquets (clip boards, thin rigid files, small cutting boards)
● masking tape to mark court limits

Rules >>

● players toss for who starts serving

● players may play standing or seated

● new balls must be introduced at every new set

● players must change ends every set and be able to excuse this plausibly to any manager who asks why

● cursing, swearing, and bratty behavior is compulsory

Officials >>
● umpire/scorekeeper (who must stand where he/she can see both players)
● ballboys/girls

Level of fitness >>

	high
✓	med
	low

WM stat >>

British companies over 200 years old may play a more idiosyncratic version, Real Tennis, however, this requires ancient offices with unusual ceiling configuration and cunningly hidden wall cabinets.

ball games

High-Shelf Volleyball

Classic volleyball using a free-standing high shelving unit as the net. This is usually played in storeroom or basement. Extra points are awarded for the player who comes up with the most ingenious reason for having to go there so often.

Object >> To hit ball (made from padded envelopes) over the net (shelf) between two teams of four persons. A point is scored every time one team gets the ball over the net or the opposing team misses. First team to reach 25 points with a minimum lead of 2 points wins.

Players >> four to six (mixed or single gender) per team on the court, but can have an unlimited squad to field substitutes whenever the team rotates after winning a serve so that workers can appear at their desks in a convincing manner.

Court >> rectangular space divided in center by a high shelf; boundary line marked in tape (30 ft x 15 ft)

Equipment >>
● volleyball made from padded envelope stuffed with shredded resumés
● masking tape to mark out court boundaries

Rules >>

● teams must volley to decide serve

● teams will rotate each time they win a serve

● ball may be served underhand or overhand

● if ball lands on the top shelf and has to be brought down, the team that threw it will forfeit five points

● if the ball explodes, the game shall be deemed void and a rematch scheduled with a new ball

Officials >>
● referee
● ball technician

Level of fitness >>

✓ high	
☐ med	
☐ low	

WM stat >>

In 1984, the tense final between rival IRS teams was interrupted when FBI agents arrested both teams and all spectators, seizing the ball as evidence in high-level money laundering case.

ball games

Paper Cup Golf

This is a risky, politically charged game, because most bosses play golf (often alone in the corner office), so if you set up a tournament, they will invariably want to join in (and win). You could be seen as a brown-nosing collaborationist bootlicker lackey. On the other hand, it is a classic infiltration and destabilizing operation where the boss gets mellow and unguarded and gives away boardroom secrets. Your choice.

Object >> to get round the nine- or 18-hole course in as few strokes as possible

Players >> solo, or in a teams of two or four, taking it in turns to play

Course >> Any office space, the more varied terrain the better. Should include bunkers, water hazards and rough patches.

Equipment >>
Only bosses and true bootlickers bring in actual golf equipment.
● golf balls made of paper and rubber bands
● iron or club made from cardboard delivery tubes shaped to player's own design
● paper cups for holes

Rules >>

● each player must make their own balls and clubs

● balls must be played where they lay

● handicaps must be verified before play

● players may use only two clubs, one of which must be a putter

● damages to come out of perpetrator's department expenses

Officials >>
● course designer
● green manager
● scorekeeper

Level of fitness >>

	high
	med
✓	low

WM stat >>

In 2002, Tyler Forest, a New Jersey photocopier mechanic out on call, achieved 9 holes in one when invited (as a joke) to play by the elite Piranha Finance Group Golf Club. He was later fired.

ball games

Boss Badminton

This won't work in every office, as it depends on the boss/line manager being the kind that likes to get down with the grunts, and has a workstation on the main floor. If he/she doesn't, then a version called Annoying Colleague Badminton can be played instead.

Object >> to play an entire game of badminton over the head of your boss or the most annoying colleague in the department. Last one given notice or termination wins.

Players >> two

Court >> a row of three work cubicles with a slacker on each outside and a line manager/boss/annoying colleague in the center

Equipment >>
● shuttlecock made out of a rubber band ball with ball point pen lid "feathers" taped to it
● racquets (clipboards or files, as cubicle tennis)
● rubber bands

Rules >>

● shuttlecock must fly over the central cubicle entirely

● shuttlecock must be out of view whenever the boss looks up to see what the noise is

● if shuttlecock falls into boss's cubicle, hitter must find a way to retrieve it without being noticed

● game is abandoned if shuttlecock hits any part of the boss's body

Officials >>
● referee
● scorekeeper

Level of fitness >>

	high	
	med	
✓	low	

WM stat >>

In 1998, Harvard MBA students M.A. Forbes II and J. Roosevelt Greenspan played a three-game tournament undetected by their professor, Harvey Neat, later diagnosed as narcoleptic.

ball games

Beverage Free Throw

A discreet game that requires little equipment, can be tailored to fit the time you have available, and is a reliable hand-eye coordination training exercise for more prestigious events.

Object >> to get your ball into your opponent's drinking cup as many times as you can in an allotted time

Players >> two (mixed play is allowed)

Court >> any two standard-sized desks plus the space between them; advanced teams may elect to pay over a partition

Equipment >>
● each player's personal drinking mug*
● small balls made from shredded memos and Scotch tape

* tournaments are played with standard paper cups, stacked in twos

Rules >>

● cups must be half filled with cooled beverage of choice

● a clean swish is 2 points; rimshots are 1 point

● players may play two halves of 15 minutes each, or if time is short, players can decide a more decisive victory by shooting best out of 5

● balls may not be replaced at any point during a single game

● cups must be at least 10 ft apart

● players must rise from their chair when shooting

Officials >>
● referee
● scorekeeper

Level of fitness >>

☐ high
☐ med
✓ low

WM stat >>

Graphic designer Milton "Air" Bodoni held the Free Throw record for three consecutive seasons (1993–5) but was later disqualified for oversugaring his beverage to handicap his opponents' balls.

ball games

Pushpin Baseball

A subversive event disguised as a progress chart that can be played under the eyes of any manager, even in meetings, because as we know, no one ever looks at progress charts.

• •

Object >> Play a game of baseball using a marked board, two teams of pushpins, and dice. This is the old-school version—you can also play this using spreadsheets on the office intranet.

Players >> two (one for each team)

Field >> the diamond (either on a computer screen or bulletin board) can be small or large but must be in proportion to the real thing.

Equipment >>
For the old-school version:
● two teams of nine pushpins (two colors)
● bulletin board with baseball diamond and positions indicated,
● two six-sided dice, one for each team

Rules >>

● regular baseball rules apply; six- to nine-inning games, depending on level of management scrutiny

● batter must first throw a single six-sided die to decide at-bat, 1–2=strike, 3–4=ball, 5–6=ball in play

● if the batter rolls 5 or 6, he/she must roll a second die to decide the result of the ball in play: 1-single, 2=double. 3=triple, 4–5=batter out, 6=home run

Officials >>
● umpire
● pushpin wrangler

Level of fitness >>

	high
	med
✓	low

WM stat >>

The glorious season enjoyed by the titanic Monsanto White Collars in 1996 (unbeaten in 162 games and World Series winners) remains the benchmark. Shoeless Ed Kropotnik, Monsanto's very own Sultan of Swat, hit 483 home runs.

ball games

Trashcan Pool

An office version of 9-ball pool. It takes a lot of setting up and is hard to disguise as work, so best played on a night or weekend shift.

Object >> to sink the nine ball, this can be achieved at any point in game play, however, cue ball has to always first hit the lowest numbered ball on the table

Players >> two individuals or 2 teams of 2

Equipment >>
● six paper cups for pockets
● double-sided tape to stick the cups to the desk
● nine balls made from warning memos and dismissal notices colored and numbered: 1 (yellow), 2 (blue), 3 (red), 4 (purple), 5 (orange), 6 (green), 7 (brown), 8 (black), 9 (yellow and white), plus a white cue ball
● one cardboard-tube billiard cue per player

Table >> standard rectangular desk, cleared of all objects with six paper cup pockets, one at each corner, one at the center of each long side of the desk

Rules >>

● balls must be of uniform size and weight

● first to win five, seven, or nine games determines the winner (depending on length of night shift)

● the cue ball must hit the lowest numbered ball before striking any other ball or a foul is committed

● three fouls and you are out unless opponent fails to warn you after second foul

Officials >>
● none: this is a game of honor

Level of fitness >>

	high
	med
✓	low

WM stat >>

The longest match ever to take place was played by the staff at Joliet Correctional Center, Illinois. Started in 1998, and interrupted by shift changes and breakouts, the game was still undecided when the center closed in 2002, and the competition was declared void.

ball games

Off-ice Hockey

An energetic, high-risk game that can result in workplace injury—and a slacker's opportunity to collect workers' compensation, if you dare to pull it off.

Object >> players must skate around the rink on chairs and use their sticks to propel the puck into the opponent's goal; team with most goals scored over three equal sessions (20 mins maximum) wins

Players >> two teams of 5 players each, one whom is the goalkeeper. If you have a small company, you can play three on a side.

Equipment >>
● office chairs with wheels, armrests removed; one for each player and for each official
● roll of masking tape or electric tape for puck
● padded-envelope body armor and helmets

Rink >> You need a large shiny surface, so use the reception or the boardroom. Erect goals at either end out of stackable chairs, mark the central face-off spot and the edge of the play area. Designate a penalty box.

● hockey sticks (cardboard tubes bent to shape, reinforced with duct tape)
● stackable chairs to form goals
● masking tape to mark edge of rink

Rules >>

● sticks must not go above shoulder height

● players (with the exception of the goalie) must not use hands to move the puck

● games are played over three equal sessions (20 mins maximum)

● zero tolerance for stick-on-body incidents

● bodychecking is allowed

● penalties given according to standard hockey rules

Officials >>
● one referee, two linesmen, all on chairs; first aid provider

Level of fitness >>

✓	high
	med
	low

WM stat >>

The most feared off-ice hockey team ever is the Wells Fargo Werewolves of Minneapolis. During an interdepartmental play off, two passing Fedex agents were concussed by flying pucks and the reception aquarium was smashed.

ball games

Office Football

An all-seated version of the great game. IT departments like to play this on-screen, but the classic is played with a padded envelope ball. The whole office gets to play this democratic version, because positions are allotted by random draw.

Object >> to score as many points as possible with touchdowns or field goals, and to prevent the other side from doing the same

Players >> two teams; 11 team members from each in play at any one time; there can be up to 46 slackers on the team

Equipment >>
● ball (made from padded envelopes)
● masking tape to mark grid and end zones
● numbered lots to draw positions

Field >> any large open plan office; divide the whole room into the gridiron; works best if desks in rows and there are very low or no partitions, so that opposing teams can intercept play. End zones must be clearly marked.

Rules >>

● play will be over four 15-minute sessions; these can be spread out over the week if management disrupts the game

● players may kick, throw or stand up, and walk or run with the ball to a teammate or to the end zone to score a touchdown or a field goal

● tries may be kicked or thrown

● opposing team may intercept throws, and tackle a player who is walking or running with the ball

● jumping on desks allowed

● if a team member is taken off the field for work purposes, there can be no substitution

Officials >>
● referee
● two line judges
● coach
● waterboy

Level of fitness >>

□ high
☑ med
□ low

WM stat >>

The NOFL (National Office Football League) was set up in 2003 with an HQ in Billings, Montana. Currently there are 3573 teams in the league divided into six IRS-inspired sections.

ball games

Office Dodgeball

A bureaucratic version of the popular children's ball game, without the balls. Office Dodgeball is a year-round game, and in some offices it is played continuously, unnoticed by management.

Object >> you and your team work to get members of the opposing team blamed for your mess-ups; if you play Sawyer's Rules you get additional points for "dodging" tasks and getting the other team to do them.

Players >> two teams of more than two but less than 10

Equipment >>
● guile and cunning
● quick reactions
● high mendacity factor

Arena >> Any office large enough to field two teams (usually rival departments) with enough staff to act as spectators and support either faction. Cheerleaders are optional.

Rules >>

● players may make deliberate mess-up to get points

● extra points are awarded for blindsiding

● three impasses (when all members of both teams have successfully dodged consequences shall be declared a tie)

● blaming that results in the firing of any team member is a professional foul, and the perpetrating team will be benched for the season

Officials >>
● scorekeeper

Level of fitness >>

	high
	med
✓	low

WM stat >>

Still undisputed champions are the DC Sidesteppers, a team of presidential aides in the Nixon administration, who never took the blame for anything and delegated every single task assigned to them.

ball games

Squash

A fun version of the elitist alpha male competitive cardiac event played by overachieving executive jackals. This is an inclusive game, and has led to many office romances.

Object >> to get as many staffers as possible into the smallest office/elevator in the building and stay there for 10 seconds; smaller offices can use a cupboard instead.

Players >> unlimited, but must be more than six

Equipment >>
- elevator, small offices, cabinets
- supply of bottled water
- cellphones for emergency communication
- lubricant (optional)

Court >> As above; choose your squash space according to staffing levels. You may run several games at once if you have the facilities

Rules >>

● packer may call for additional staff over the office intercom using a previously agreed code

● claustrophobes must bring in a note from their physician

● packing should be done by size and weight

● players with communicable disease should be benched

● number of staff and dimensions of the squash space must be posted onto www.officesquashleague.com for evaluation

● fatalities mean disqualification and a lifelong ban

Officials >>
● lead packer (preferably a Tetris major)
● assistant packers
● maintenance engineer

Level of fitness >>

	high
✓	med
	low

WM stat >>

In 2004, 103 staffers were packed into the 6 ft x 4 ft x 10 ft office of the Assistant Secretary to the Deputy Assistant Manager to the Administration Manager (Stationery) of the Federal Communications Commission in Milwaukee.

ball games

The Workers' Manifesto
Official Certificate

This is to certify that

....

of

....

has successfully partaken in a minimum of three events from
all four categories and is therefore a recognized
Slacker (1st Class)

Waste *Their* Time, Not Yours